The 10-Minutes DIY Homemade Face Mask

A Step by Step Beginners Guide to Make Your Own Protective, Washable, and Reusable Cloth Face Mask With Illustrations Included

By

Dr. Lee Henton

Copyright © 2020 – Dr. Lee Henton

All rights reserved

No part of this publication may be reproduced, distributed, or transmitted in any form or by any means, including photocopying, recording, or other electronic or mechanical methods, without the prior written permission of the publisher, except in the case of brief quotations embodied in reviews and certain other non-commercial uses permitted by copyright law.

Disclaimer

This publication is designed to provide reliable information on the subject matter only for educational purposes, and it is not intended to provide medical advice for any medical treatment. You should always consult your doctor or physician for guidance before you stop, start, or alter any prescription medications or attempt to implement the methods discussed. This book is published independently by the author and has no affiliation with any brands or products mentioned within it. The author hereby disclaims any responsibility or liability whatsoever that is incurred from the use or application of the contents of this publication by the purchaser or reader. The purchaser or reader is hereby responsible for his or her own actions.

Credits: Cover image designed from resources at Freepik.com

Books By The Same Author

No	Title
1	The Secrets of Vagus Nerve Stimulation
A Special Do-It-Yourself Homemade Guide to Protect You From Viruses and Bacteria	
2	The 5-Minutes DIY Homemade Hand Sanitizer
3	DIY Homemade Hand Sanitizer and Homemade Face Mask (2 Books In 1)
Other Books Co-written By The Author	
4	The Budget-Friendly Renal Diet Cookbook

Table of Contents

Books By The Same Author 3

About The Author 7

Introduction 8

Chapter 1 12

The ABC of Face Mask 12

    What is Face Mask 13

    Types of Face Mask and Recommendations For Usage ... 13

        N95 Respirator 14

        Medical (Surgical) Face Mask 16

        Homemade Cloth Face Mask 18

    Are Face Masks Effective Against Virus Infection? 19

    Why You Should Make Your Own Face Mask 23

    Reusing and Disposing of Face Mask 24

Chapter 2 31

DIY Homemade Face Mask 31

    Best Fabrics For Reusable Homemade Mask 31

    Are Fabric Face Masks Really Effective? 32

Are Coffee Filters, Paper Towels, and Tissues Effective? 33

Making Homemade Face Mask 34

Sewing Method 34

    List of Materials and Tools 35

    Step 1: Measurement and Cut List 35

    Step 2: Fold and Sew Along The Top Edge 37

    Step 3: Pin Elastic or Fabric Ties 39

    Step 4: Sew The Sides To Secure The Elastic or Ties 40

    Step 5: Insert a Metal Wire For Nose Cover 41

    Step 6: Make The Pleats 41

    Step 7: Insert The Filter 43

No-Sewing "Emergency" Method 44

    List of Materials 44

    Step 1: Prepare Your Fabric 45

    Step 2: Make The First and Second Folds 45

    Step 3: Fold The Ends of the Fabric 46

    Step 4: Insert The Rubber Bands 46

    Step 5: Lift The Mask to Your Face 47

Chapter 3 49

Best Practice For Handling Face Mask 49
    Wearing Face Masks The Right Way 49
    Removing Face Masks The Right Way 52
Conclusion 54
References 56

About The Author

Dr. Lee Henton is a US-trained General Practice Doctor from the Johns Hopkins University School of Medicine with additional qualification in nutritional medicine from Iowa State University. He is a certified specialist in dietology and nutrition.

He has extensive years of medical and nutritional experience across general medicine, pediatrics, traumatology, addictions, food nutrition, and diet therapy.

He currently runs a co-established private medical and wellness practice where he operates from. His approach is personalized with each client by combining medical and food nutrition counseling. All advice he provides is at par with his experience, as well as with medical and nutritional concepts. He specializes primarily in men and women's health.

He lives in Minnesota with his wife and two daughters.

Introduction

It is no surprise that homemade face masks have now become an essential global commodity amidst the current global pandemic crises, most especially after the WHO and CDC changed its guidelines that required that everyone should wear some form of cloth face-covering when moving around in public places to prevent the spread of COVID-19. This announcement has resulted in a surge of consumers swooping in on supermarkets and online stores to purchase face masks, most notably, the medical face masks and the N95 respirators, which are both reserved for use by healthcare professionals. This has led to an increased scarcity of this all too important commodity, which is mostly needed in hospitals, thus calling for consumers to seek out alternative measures in making their own face masks from home. As a result of the ever-increasing demand for face masks, the internet has thus become awash with several Do-It-Yourself homemade face mask guides, many of which do not take into cognizance the recommended fabrics and steps that must be adhered if the aim is to protect the wearer from the coronavirus. Nonetheless, it is surprisingly easy to make a DIY face mask using materials you most likely have at home; however, not everyone has the experience in using the sewing machine to make a face mask, and if this is you, then not to worry because this book does not only cater for people with experience in using the sewing machine but also people with no experience using the sewing machine, threads and needle. With this book, simplified using the most easy-to-understand language, you are on your way to making your own face mask in 10 minutes or less from the comfort of your home even if you have no clue where to start from.

At the end of this book, you will:

- Gain a deeper understanding of what face mask is and its importance against viruses and toxic particles.
- Be enlightened on the different types of face masks used for protection against COVID-19, the efficacy of each type of masks against virus infections, as well as when and who should use them.
- Know how face masks work in protecting you from viruses and toxic particles.
- Understand the real benefits of making your own face mask from home.
- Know the best fabrics to use if you want to make a reusable homemade face mask.
- Know why you should not use some of the commonly recommended fabrics for your face mask.
- Uncover all you need to get started in making your own face mask with the sewing and no-sewing methods, such as the material lists, measurements and cut list in inches for adults

and kids, as well as the step by step instructions to follow.

- Be familiar with the best practice for handling face mask, either when wearing or removing a face mask to stay protected against the viruses and toxic particles that you mask may habor without your knowledge.

…and much more.

So, without further ado, let's begin proper

Chapter 1

The ABC of Face Mask

In late 2019, a novel coronavirus emerged in China, which has since spread rapidly throughout the world. This novel coronavirus is called severe acute respiratory syndrome coronavirus 2 (SARS-CoV-2), and the disease that it causes is called coronavirus disease, colloquially called COVID-19.

While it is common for people with COVID-19 to experience light illness, others may also experience difficulty in breathing, respiratory failure or even pneumonia. It is known that older individuals, as well as people with underlying health conditions, are at higher risk for severe illness from COVID-19. It is to this effect that the World Health Organization (WHO) and the Centers for Disease Control and Prevention (CDC) have called for the practice of safe health against this disease, one of such being the use of face masks to prevent infection, others are regular handwashing with soap and water or in its absence, the use of hand sanitizer as well practicing social distancing.

What is Face Mask

Face masks are one tool used for curbing the spread of diseases. They are loose-fitting masks that typically cover the nose and mouth, with ear loops, ties or bands behind the head.

Face mask protects the nose and mouth of the wearer from splashes or sprays of body fluids. When a person coughs, talks or even sneezes, there is the tendency that tiny drops of such can be released into the atmosphere, with the potential to infect others. Wearing a face mask by someone who is ill can reduce the number of germs that are released, thus protecting other people from becoming sick.

But, are face masks really that effective, and if yes, when should it be worn and by who?

Read on to learn the answers to this question and more.

Types of Face Mask and Recommendations For Usage

When you hear of COVID-19 prevention face masks, there are generally three types of such masks recognized by the WHO and CDC.

Let us explore each of them in a bit more detail below.

N95 Respirator

A respirator is a personal protective equipment (PPE), which, when worn, prevents health hazards, such as inhaling of aerosol particles (e.g., dust, mist, and smoke). It also provides protection to the wearer from airborne infectious agents such as viruses and bacteria, an example of which are the coronavirus, H1N1, SARS, etc. An example of such a respirator is the N95, which is a more tight-fitting face mask, capable of not only filtering out 95 percent of microscopic particles, but also, splashes, sprays, and large droplets, including viruses and bacteria. This type of mask is not meant for use by the general public. They are to be worn:

- Exclusively by health care professionals attending to patients having respiratory infections such as cough and cold as well as patients under investigation.
- While entering rooms of confirmed or suspected COVID-19 patients.

- While retrieving clinical specimens, or soiled medical supplies and equipment or whenever a health care professional come in contact with potentially contaminated environmental surfaces.

This respirator is generally oval in shape and designed to provide a tight seal to your face, with elastic bands helping to hold it to your face firmly. Some types may include an exhalation valve as an attachment to help with breathing and the buildup of heat and humidity.

N95 respirators are not one-size-fits-all and must be fit-tested before usage to ensure a proper seal is formed, else, you won't receive adequate protection. And even after being fit-tested, wearers of N95 respirators must always perform a seal check any time they put one on.

For respirators to be used for commercial consumption, they must meet the NIOSH (National Institute for Occupational Safety and Health) standards in the US, and the European standard EN 149: 2001 in Europe.

Medical (Surgical) Face Mask

Medical face masks are a disposable medical device and loose-fitting masks that provide cover for your nose, mouth, and chin, thus:

- Protecting you from sprays, splashes and large-particle droplets
- Preventing the spread of potentially infectious secretions of the respiratory tract from the wearer to others

When a medical mask is worn by a caregiver, the patient and his or her environment (air, surfaces, surgical site, etc.) are protected. Studies conducted shows that medical professional using medical face masks correctly are 80% less risky of being infected than those who don't. On the other hand, when a contagious patient wears it, the patient is prevented from contaminating his or her surroundings and environment.

Medical masks come in different designs but are often flat and rectangular in shape with folds, and with a metal strip at its top that can be formed to your nose.

Medical masks are supported by elastic bands or long, straight ties that keep the mask in place while it's worn, which are either looped to the back of the ears or tied around the head.

For medical masks to be used for commercial consumption, they must comply with the United States American Society for Testing and Materials (ASTM) standards, and in Europe, it must satisfy the European standard EN 14683

Both the N95 respirators and medical masks are critical supplies that the CDC recommends to be reserved for healthcare workers that work with infectious patients. However, this is not the case, as it is evident that the rapid spread of COVID-19 throughout the world has led many people to purchase medical masks to keep at home, in addition to the imbalance in the demand and supply of N95 respirators. These gaps have resulted in the making of homemade face mask as an alternative and additional measure of protection from the virus.

Homemade Cloth Face Mask

To curb the spread of coronavirus by people without symptoms, the CDC now recommends that everyone wears cloth face masks, such as homemade face masks while in public places where social distancing of up to six-feet is difficult to maintain, e.g. supermarkets and pharmacies. This recommendation is alongside the continued adherence to proper hygiene practices.

Healthcare workers who make use of homemade face masks as opposed to N95 respirators or surgical masks are advised to apply extreme caution, which is recommended to be used in combination with a face shield covering the whole front and sides of the face and extending to the chin or below.

Two ways wearing a face mask helps prevent people from being infected are:

- By blocking the inhalation of the virus through most airborne droplets.
- By preventing the wearer from touching their mouths and noses.

Are Face Masks Effective Against Virus Infection?

SARS-CoV-2 can be spread from person to person through small respiratory droplets, which are generated when a person infected with the virus exhales, coughs, or sneezes. A person can then contract this virus when these droplets are breathed in. Also, respiratory droplets housing the virus can be transferred to several objects or surfaces. When these contaminated objects or surfaces are touched, and you thereafter touch your eyes, nose, or mouth, it can also lead to infection.

But does wearing a face mask help prevent the spread of viruses, such as the flu or SARS-CoV-2?

Let's take a look at what the experts have to say on this subject.

In the case of COVID-19, the CDC mentions that simple face coverings or masks can lower its spread, thus recommending that people should wear a cloth face covering to cover their nose and mouth when in a public setting, and also recommends healthcare workers wear face masks when handling with patients with the flu. This is in addition to social distancing, regular hand cleaning or hand washing and other everyday preventive actions.

Additionally, a study conducted in 2013 looked at how face masks could help limit the spread of seasonal flu from infected persons when they exhale small droplets housing the virus. In all, it was found that wearing face masks resulted in more than a threefold reduction in how much virus was sprayed into the air by infected persons.

Another study that was analyzed from the data of thousands of Japanese schoolchildren found that vaccination and wearing a face mask reduced the likelihood of contracting seasonal influenza. And more importantly, researchers discovered that the rate of contracting the flu was reduced when face masks were worn alongside proper hand hygiene. This thus leads to the conclusion that although face masks help reduce the spread of flu and the coronavirus, regular washing of the hands remains an essential element in stopping the spread of the viruses. That being said, are all face masks then equally effective at preventing the spread of viruses such as the coronavirus? Let's have a look at the recommendations from experts per the effectiveness of the three major types of face masks against the novel coronavirus.

N95 Respirator

N95 respirator masks certified for use by the CDC and NIOSH, are designed to protect the wearer from large and small particles in the air, such as viruses as well as smaller respiratory droplets, such as those containing SARS-CoV-2. The name stems from the fact that they can filter 95 percent of airborne particles, according to the CDC. They are also used when painting or handling likely toxic materials.

N95 masks are mostly used by healthcare workers to protect them against airborne infectious diseases, most notably, the COVID-19. Unlike the regular face masks such as medical masks, respirators protect against large and small particles. Overall, N95 masks are considered more effective at preventing the spread of the flu and coronavirus when compared to medical face masks.

For N95 respirators to be effective at preventing viruses, it must form a perfect seal so that no gaps can allow airborne viruses to pass through.

Medical Mask

Medical (surgical) face masks are relatively loose-fitting, disposable masks approved for use by the Food and Drug Administration (FDA) as medical devices, and which are often worn by doctors, dentists, and nurses while treating patients.

These masks prevent the escape of large droplets of bodily fluids (that may house viruses or other germs) via the nose and mouth. Likewise, they protect against splashes and sprays from other persons, e.g., those from sneezes and coughs. However, the average masks bought at the local drugstore are insufficient to filter out viruses in tiny droplets. For example, medical masks can't protect a person from being infected with SARS-CoV-2. Medical masks do not filter out smaller aerosol particles, and even so, as you inhale, air leakage via the sides of the mask occurs.

For this purpose, experts recommend special masks with a fine mesh capable of capturing microscopic organisms that have to be worn correctly for them to work.

It is important to note when airborne virus particles, from a cough or sneeze, comes in contact with your eyes, masks worn over the face would be unable to protect you from such viruses.

Homemade Cloth Face Mask

Homemade cloth face masks used in public settings don't provide the same level of protection as N95 respirators and medical face masks but only offer a small degree of protection. However, when worn by the broader public, they can help reduce the community spread of viruses. This is because they help protect others from being infected by your respiratory droplets (such as sneezes and coughs) if you acquired the coronavirus but without symptoms and vice versa.

The CDC recommends that in addition to using homemade face masks in public settings, social distancing and proper hygiene should likewise be practiced.

Why You Should Make Your Own Face Mask

- Making your own face mask from the availability of common materials can be made at the

convenience of your home in unlimited supply, especially when you become sick, which will help provide some level of protection to friends and family while you seek medical advice
- Making your own face mask, as well as for family and friends, would help decrease the demand for limited supplies of commercial medical face masks, which are critically needed by hospitals and nursing homes.
- Homemade face masks can lower the risk of people without symptoms from transmitting the virus via speaking, coughing, or sneezing.
- Homemade face masks, when done right is washable and reusable, thus making them environmentally friendly.

Reusing and Disposing of Face Mask

Most face masks, by best practice, are designed for one-time use only. Ideally, once a face mask is soiled, or the inner lining becomes moist, such a mask should no longer be used because rarely can they be sterilized for reuse. For example, the WHO recommends that a single-use mask be removed once it is damp from your breath and never reuse it. Under normal circumstances, such masks are disposed of when an infected patient has been tended to by a healthcare professional. However, due to the dwindling supply of face masks, and if you need to use a face mask either because you are sick or taking care of a sick person, then face masks can be reused under certain conditions.

The procedures below details how to reuse and dispose of a face mask across the three major types of COVID-19 face mask.

Medical Face Mask

The CDC, in a bid to address the shortage of face masks, released a guideline that addresses the reusability of face masks. One of such is that a medical mask should be used only by the same person and not shared amongst medical professionals, and when not in use, such a mask be stored in a breathable container, like a paper bag. Also, extra measures, as given below, can be taken to further ensure a medical face mask can be reused, given the shortages in its availability.

If the mask is dry and its layers and shape remains intact, it can then be reused for three days. To reuse a medical face mask, simply put it in a zip lock pouch with a desiccated gel. The purpose of the gel is to absorb the moisture, thus keeping the mask dry. On the other hand, if it has been worn by an infected person, it should never be reused but immediately discarded.

N95 Respirator

According to the CDC guidelines, it is better to wear the respirator for an extended period (such as the whole shift) instead of taking it off then putting it back on. This is because it reduces the number of people touching their faces, which potentially allows the virus to enter their body. It also recommends a clean and breathable container such as a paper bag for storing the N95 respirators, which is to be regularly disposed of, so they don't contaminate your mask later on. The guidelines, however, provide no safe amount of reuses, leaving medical professionals to apply their judgment. Nonetheless, additional steps can be taken to preserve and reuse N95 respirators, as given below.

N95 respirators are to be stored in a closed plastic container when not in use with regular cleansing of the storage container. For the N95 respirator to be reused, a number of steps can be taken.

- The used respirator can be left in the dry atmosphere for about 3-4 days to dry out. The reason for this is that coronavirus requires a host in other to survive. It can survive for up to 48hours on a metal surface, for 72 hours on plastic, and for 72 hours on cardboard. Thus, if the respirator is left to dry for about 3-4 days, the virus would not survive.
- Another way is sterilizing the N95 respirator is by hanging it in the oven (without contacting metal) using a wooden clip for about 30 min at 70 degrees Celsius.

N95 respirators that adhere to the above procedure can be used up to a maximum of 5 times, or alternatively, follow the guidelines made available by the manufacturer.

On the other hand, N95 respirators are to be immediately discarded if:

- It is used during aerosol-generating procedures, i.e., procedures such as coughing, that cause the

release of airborne particles, which can result in the spread of respiratory infections.
- It is contaminated with blood, nasal or respiratory secretions, or other bodily fluids from patients.
- The wearer came in close contact with any patient infected with an infectious disease.

Homemade Cloth Face Mask

A 2015 study published in the medical journal BMJ Open, advised against the medical use of cloth masks, in contrast with disposable ones. This reason for this is that moisture retention, poor filtration, as well as the reuse of cloth masks could result in an increased risk of healthcare workers being infected. However, individuals using their own cloth masks are required to wash them after each use or regularly machine-wash them. Nonetheless, you should be aware that using a homemade cloth face mask would only be marginally effective at preventing the spread of infectious disease when compared with a medical face mask or an N95 respirator. Still, it is better than having no protection at all.

The WHO also mentioned that heat of 133°F could kill the coronavirus, meaning if you are using a homemade face mask made from cloth, it should be washed properly and frequently after each use with detergent and water, then having it air-dried. This would make such masks reusable after it has been worn.

A Short message from the Author:

Hey, I hope you are enjoying the book? I would love to hear your thoughts!

Many readers do not know how hard reviews are to come by and how much they help an author.

I would be incredibly grateful if you could take just 60 seconds to write a short review on the product page of this book, even if it is a few sentences!

Thanks for the time taken to share your thoughts!

Your review will genuinely make a difference for me and help gain exposure for my work.

Chapter 2

DIY Homemade Face Mask

Given the current shortage of face masks such as the medical face masks and N95 respirators, which by the way, are reserved for health care professionals, most people have thus been forced to seek out ways in creating homemade face masks with anything from cloth to scarves and bandanas.

Although homemade face masks made from cotton woven fabric are about one-third as effective as medical masks in preventing infection, they are still capable of reducing the number of germs spread by the wearer significantly.

Best Fabrics For Reusable Homemade Mask

Right off the bat, the best fabric for homemade masks is a tightly woven, 100% cotton fabric such as bedsheets, woven shirts, curtains, or fabric from pillowcases, which are all great options if made totally from cotton. If you have clothing or bedding items at home that are still in good condition, they can be used rather than having to buy new fabric.

On the other hand, it is recommended to avoid knit jersey and T-shirt fabrics, simply because they create holes when stretched, which could allow the virus to pass through.

Besides a pure 100% cotton fabric, a non-fusible nonwoven interface fabric for the filter pocket can also be used. This is also needed to provide an extra layer to block out particles. However, if unavailable, the nonwoven fabric can be substituted for a high-efficiency particulate air (HEPA) vacuum bag filter without fiberglass, which is also good for filtering particles. Still, you must ensure that the HEPA filter is one that is washable and reusable else, you will always have to replace the filters each time you wear the mask.

Are Fabric Face Masks Really Effective?

Yes and no.

The CDC advises the use of N95 respirators for the best protection but notes that bandana or scarf be used as a last resort if hospital-approved medical masks are unavailable, especially for medical professionals.

However, at this point in the global pandemic, homemade masks are being made by the broader population as a replacement for bandanas and scarves.

According to the CDC, if you need a mask for yourself or other persons not treating COVID-19 patients, then homemade cloth masks can help minimize the spread of the coronavirus. These fabric masks help best to protect you in places such as pharmacies or grocery stores from asymptomatic persons, where it is difficult to maintain a six-feet distance from other shoppers and works best if worn by everyone else.

Are Coffee Filters, Paper Towels, and Tissues Effective?

Even though the CDC guidelines for DIY homemade face masks incorporate a coffee filter, Nate Favini, a board-certified internist, remarks that coffee filters, paper towels, and tissues (even in layers) are not very effective at filtering out microscopic particles. Besides, they cants also be washed, thus making it impossible for a face mask made of these materials to be reused. However, this does not imply they can't be used if it so happens to be the only materials at your disposal.

Aside from the weak filtration property of the coffee filters, they can quickly become saturated with moisture, making face masks made with any of these paper materials suitable only for one-time use only. That being said, subsequent sections on making homemade face masks would focus on fabrics that can be washed and reused.

Making Homemade Face Mask

In subsequent sections, I would discuss in a simple fashion how you can make your own face masks either by sewing or no-sewing methods, especially for those who aren't a seamstress or a seamster.

So, without further ado, let's begin.

Sewing Method

Research shows that the most effective masks are made of two layers of tightly woven cotton fabric, with an internal pocket filter where additional layers of filtration material can be added if desired. The method described below satisfies this study.

List of Materials and Tools

- 100% tightly woven cotton fabric
- Elastic or fabric ties (to make strips, use the same cotton fabric, or pre-made bias binding, or strips of cotton jersey) for the ear loop to keep the mask secure on the face
- Nonfusible nonwoven interface filter fabric for an extra layer of protection (or HEPA filter) – optional
- Pipe cleaner, floral wire, or other flexible metal wire for nose cover – optional
- Scissors
- Measuring tape
- Pins or clips
- Sewing machine and thread

Instructions

Step 1: Measurement and Cut List

Cotton fabric:

- For adult-sized, cut the fabric into one rectangular shape at 16" long and 8.5" wide
- For child-sized, cut the fabric into one rectangular shape at 14" long and 6.5" wide

Elastic:

- For adult-sized, cut 2 pieces of 7" long (or 8" for larger adult size) elastic ear loop
- For child-sized, cut 2 pieces of 6" long elastic ear loop

Fabric ties, if elastic are not used:

- Cut 4 rectangular pieces of fabric ties each at 18" long and 1.75" wide. If 18" is too long for some people, you can adjust the length accordingly.
- Fold the long sides so that it meets in the middle, then fold again in half to encase the raw edges. To create the ties, stitch down the length of the rectangles along the edge, as shown below.

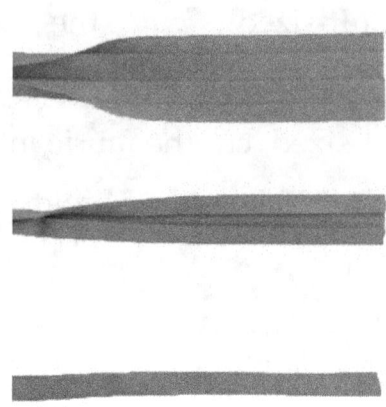

Step 2: Fold and Sew Along The Top Edge

- Fold the rectangle cotton fabric into half, with the right sides facing each other as shown below

- Sew along the top edge of width 8.5", by using a 5/8" seam (a line where two pieces of fabric are sewn together) allowance and leave a 4" opening at the center of the seam (marked with pins as shown above) for the filter pocket, and to allow the mask to be turned right side out after sewing.

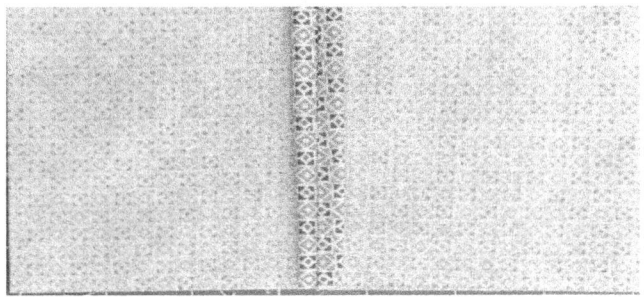

- Turn the fabric so that the seam is centered in the middle of one side, then fold the excess seam allowance under to encase the raw edge of the fabric, then topstitch (as shown below) along the sides of the seam for a neater edge. This is to help prevent the fraying of the fabric when filters are inserted and removed.

Note: When topstitching, ensure not to mistakenly stitch the 4" opening at the center of the seam.

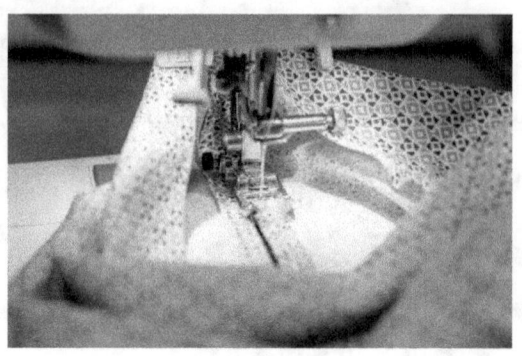

Step 3: Pin Elastic or Fabric Ties

If Using Elastic:

- Sandwich the elastic pieces between the two layers of the fabric, then pin one end of the elastic to the top and the other end to the bottom of the sides of the fabric rectangle. This will create the elastic earloop on the outside immediately the mask is turned right side out and pleated.
- Repeat this process on each side to make two ear loops.

If Using Fabric Ties:

- If no elastic is available, 4 fabric ties, one in each corner, with each one being 18" long, can likewise be used. One tie in each of the 4 corners should then be sewn. Caution should be applied so as not to catch the ties or the elastic pieces in the side seams when sewing them.

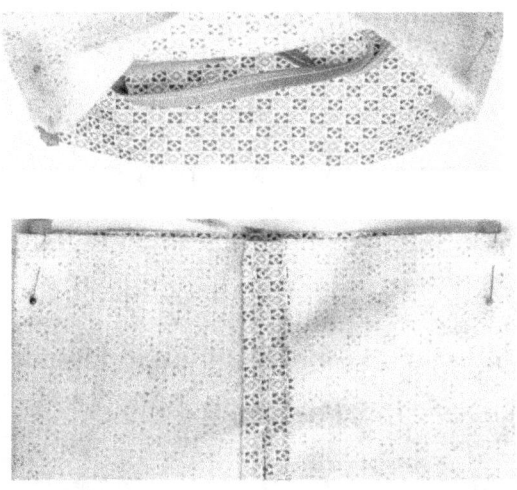

Step 4: Sew The Sides To Secure The Elastic or Ties

- Using a 3/8" seam allowance, sew the sides of the facemask, backstitch over the elastic or fabric ties to secure them, then trim the corners of the face mask with scissors to make it easier to turn the mask right side out. Be careful not to clip the stitches mistakenly.

- Turn the mask right side out and press with an iron.

Step 5: Insert a Metal Wire For Nose Cover

- For the mask to fit properly around your nose, cut a 6" piece of pipe cleaner, floral wire, or other flexible wire to make a nose cover.
- Insert the wire via the pocket opening before forming the pleats, and slide it to the very top of the mask. Topstitch around the sides of the wire to keep it in place.

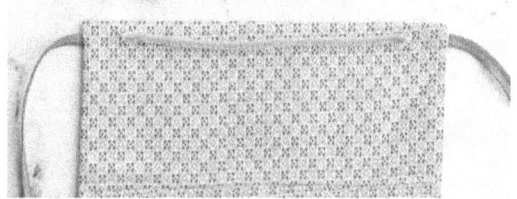

Step 6: Make The Pleats

- Use a pen to mark the mask with three evenly spaced lines, and use the lines to create evenly spaced 1/2" pleats. Use pins to hold down the folds and ensure all the pleats are facing the same direction.

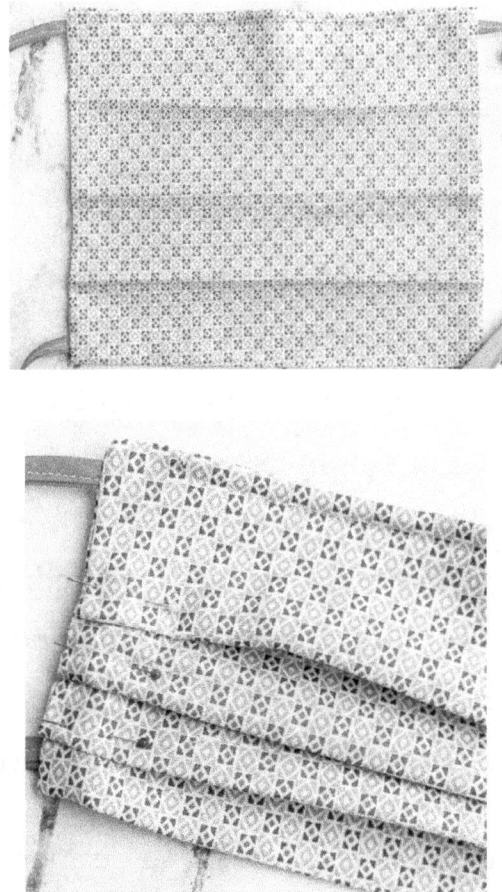

- Sew along the sides of the pleats to secure them. This ensures the pleats open downwards when the mask is worn, thus stopping any particles from being collected into the fold pockets.

Step 7: Insert The Filter

- Make a filter for the mask using a non-fusible nonwoven interfacing or HEPA filter without fiberglass. How big this filter would be depends on the size of the filter pocket opening. Cut out the appropriate shape and fit it inside the filter pocket of your mask until it fits in smoothly.
- All the areas that you will need to breathe through should be well covered. The filter does not need to go all through the under of your chin or even the area of your cheeks since the mask presses these areas against your face.

Upon making the mask, it is important that it is sterilized by washing with detergent and water, using a washing machine, or by boiling it in water to kill any inherent germs. Then allow it to dry out either by sun-drying or hanging it in an area with good airflow.

No-Sewing "Emergency" Method

Making a no-sew face mask is easier than you may be thinking, and a convenient substitute if you can not sew or do not have the proper materials. The no-sew method does not require you to be crafty or to have experience in using the needle and thread. The good news is it takes about 5 minutes to make, all from the supplies you most likely have at home. I have included potential substitutions in the following demonstration should incase you don't have the suggested items.

So, let's begin.

List of Materials

- 100% tightly woven cotton fabric or a cotton bandana or scarf as recommended by CDC
- Nonfusible nonwoven interface filter fabric for an extra layer of protection (or HEPA filter) – optional
- Pipe cleaner, floral wire, or other flexible metal wire – optional

- Rubber bands, hair ties, or shoelaces

Instructions

Step 1: Prepare Your Fabric

- Cut and lay out a 20"x 20" or a 22"x 22" square of cotton fabric or any of the substitutes in the material list section above. It has to be either of these measurements so that it's large enough to cover your nose and mouth.
- Lay out flat your chosen fabric on the table, with the patterned side faced down towards the table, and the backside faced upward towards you
- Place the filter in the center of the square (optional)

Step 2: Make The First and Second Folds

- For the first fold, fold the top and bottom edge of the fabric so that they converge at the center of your chosen fabric.

- Place a pipe cleaner, floral wire, or other flexible metal wire at the center of the top edge to make a nose cover (optional). This helps the mask fit properly around your nose.
- For the second fold, repeat the same process by folding the top and bottom edge of the fabric. This will create some pleats that will help make the mask fit properly on your face.

Step 3: Fold The Ends of the Fabric

- Fold both the right and left sides of your chosen fabric towards the center. A smaller rectangle of folded fabric will now be formed. This will help you to place a rubber band on both sides of the smaller rectangular fabric.

Step 4: Insert The Rubber Bands

- Slip in the rubber band at one end of the folded fabric, and another band on the other end. If using hair ties instead, loop it around the end of the fabric. And if using shoelaces, place the center

of the shoelace in the folded fabric and pull the straps tight.
- Tuck the ends of the folds into each other to secure the fabric.

Step 5: Lift The Mask to Your Face

- To wear, lift and bring the mask to your mouth, putting the bands or hair ties around your ears to have it secured. For shoelaces, it should be tied behind your head.
- Adjust the mask where necessary, and ensure both your mouth and nose are well covered

The end… almost!

Hey! We've made it to the final chapter of this book, and I hope you've enjoyed it so far.

If you have not done so yet, I would be incredibly thankful if you could take just a minute to leave a quick review on this book's product page.

Reviews are not easy to come by, and as an independent author with a little marketing budget, I rely on you, my readers, to leave a short review on my book.

Even if it is just a sentence or two!

So if you really enjoyed this book, please leave a brief review.

I truly appreciate your effort to leave your review, as it truly makes a huge difference.

Thanks once again from the depth of my heart for purchasing this book and reading it to the end

Chapter 3

Best Practice For Handling Face Mask

When a face mask becomes moist, it should be removed, replaced, or washed. Product instructions on the use and storage of face mask should always be followed, as well as the procedures on wearing and removing a face mask. If no product instructions are available for wearing and removing a face mask, then you should adhere to the guidelines below.

Wearing Face Masks The Right Way

Although face masks can help minimize the spread of the flu and other respiratory viruses, they only do so if worn correctly and regularly.

The guidelines below are to be followed for proper mask-wearing:

1. Your hands should first be cleaned with soap and water or hand sanitizer for at least 20 seconds before touching and wearing a face mask.

2. Ensure no tears or holes are found on either side of the face mask before it is worn.
3. Ensure that you figured the side of the mask that is the top. The top of the mask (typically the side that has a stiff bendable edge) is designed to adjust to the shape of your nose.
4. Ensure that you figured the side of the mask that is the front. This is because the colored side of the mask is usually the front and is designed to be worn from the outside, away from your face, with the white side touching your face. This step typically describes a medical face mask, so you need to determine the front of your homemade face mask.
5. Adjust the stiff edge of the mask to fit into the shape of your nose.
6. Pull the bottom of the mask over your mouth and chin.
7. The instructions below should be followed for the type of ear loops you are using to keep the mask secured on your face.

- Face mask with elastic earloops: Hold the mask by the ear loops, then place a loop around each ear.
- Face mask with ties: The mask should be brought to your nose level, then place the top ties around the crown of your head, securing it with a bow, and likewise, secure the bottom ties with a bow at the nape of your neck.

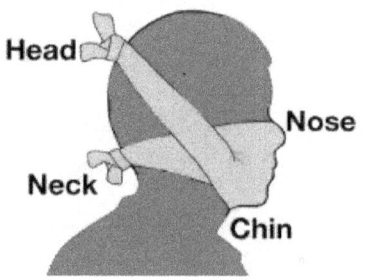

- Face mask with bands: With the mask in your hand, and with its top (the nosepiece) at your fingertips, allow the bands to freely hang below your hands. Then bring the mask to the level of your nose, and pull the top strap around your head so that it is resting over the crown of your head. Likewise, pull the bottom strap around your head so that it is resting at the nape of your neck.

8. The mask should not be touched upon being worn until it is removed, and if touched, rewash your hands or use hand sanitizer.

Removing Face Masks The Right Way

While removing a face mask, care should be applied to ensure it is being done the right way. This is because not removing the mask according to best practice puts you at risk of being infected with the flu or other respiratory virus.

The guidelines below are to be followed for proper mask-removal:

1. Your hands should be cleaned with soap and water or with a hand sanitizer before touching the mask.
2. Avoid having to touch the front of the mask, which is more likely to have been contaminated. Only the elastic ear loops, ties, or band should be touched with your hands.

3. The instructions below should be followed for the type of ear loops you are using when removing the face mask

    - Face mask with elastic earloops: Hold both of the elastic ear loops and gently lift and remove the mask.
    - Face mask with ties: The bottom bow should first be untied, followed by the top bow, then gently pull the mask away from your face as the ties are loosened.
    - Face mask with bands: The bottom strap over your head should first be lifted, then pull the top strap over your head, gently pulling the mask away.

4. Follow the procedure in this section of the book, **Reusing and Disposing of Face Mask**, after wearing a medical face mask, respirator, or a homemade cloth face mask to determine how each mask should either be reused or disposed of.
5. Clean your hands with soap and water or with hand sanitizer after discarding the face mask.

Conclusion

I'd like to thank you and congratulate you for transiting my lines from start to finish.

In this book, I have provided you with the most valid information that you need to safely make your own face mask in 10 minutes or less amidst the scarcity of face masks, which, most importantly, are reserved for healthcare professionals. Not only that, but I have also ensured that the fabrics recommended are capable of reducing the spread of the coronavirus when worn. The step by step process of making homemade face masks has also been simplified to make it easy for you to understand and follow through with. Lastly, I have shared many important tips you need in practicing safe wearing and removal of face masks, which is all but essential toward preventing yourself from the infections of viruses and toxic particles that your mask may harbor without your knowledge. Therefore, it is my sincere desire that you found great value from the invaluable and simplified insights shared in this book, which I hope you put into action right away.

Given the current global pandemic, I urge you to take full responsibility for your overall health and wellbeing.

I wish you the very best.

References

Seladi-Schulman, J., PhD. (2020, April 6). Can Face Masks Protect You from the 2019 Coronavirus? What Types, When and How to Use. Retrieved from https://www.healthline.com/health/coronavirus-mask#protection

Lexie Sachs, Good Housekeeping Institute. (2020, April 13). How to Make Face Masks for Yourself and Hospitals During the Coronavirus Shortage. Retrieved from https://www.goodhousekeeping.com/health/a31902442/how-to-make-medical-face-masks/

Coronavirus Disease 2019 (COVID-19). (2020, February 11). Retrieved from https://www.cdc.gov/coronavirus/2019-ncov/prevent-getting-sick/diy-cloth-face-coverings.html

Instructables. (2020, April 19). DIY Cloth Face Mask. Retrieved from https://www.instructables.com/id/DIY-Cloth-Face-Mask/

Sampol, C. (2020, April 15). Surgical Masks, Respirators, Barrier Masks: Which Masks Actually Protect Against Coronavirus? Retrieved from http://emag.medicalexpo.com/which-masks-actually-protect-against-coronavirus/

Barking Up The Wrong Tree - How to be awesome at life. (n.d.). Retrieved December 10, 2019, from https://www.bakadesuyo.com

Influenza Virus Aerosols in Human Exhaled Breath: Particle Size, Culturability, and Effect of Surgical Masks. (2013, March 1). Retrieved from https://www.ncbi.nlm.nih.gov/pmc/articles/PMC3591312/

Meagan Visser. (2020, March 14). Homemade Essential Oil Hand Sanitizer Recipes For Adults & Children. Retrieved from https://www.growingupherbal.com/homemade-essential-oil-hand-sanitizer/

Leiva, C. (2020, April 8). The Best Materials For DIY Face Masks And Filters. Retrieved from https://www.huffpost.com/entry/best-materials-diy-face-masks-filters_l_5e8ce4c6c5b6e1a2e0fb4ada

Holland, K. (2019, April 18). Mercury Detox: Separating Fact from Fiction. Retrieved from https://www.healthline.com/health/mercury-detox#reducing-exposure

How to Make a No-Sew Face Mask in Less Than 5 Minutes. (2020, April 10). Retrieved from https://www.thespruce.com/no-sew-mask-4801991

www.ingramcontent.com/pod-product-compliance
Lightning Source LLC
Chambersburg PA
CBHW052106110526
44591CB00013B/2366